# Graduation: Celebrate with Style!

## A Graduation Party Planning Guide

By Mary J. Anderson & Ginger Venable

Second Edition

Printed and bound in the United States of America.

To order additional copies of this book send $9.95 + $2 for shipping to Lanewood Marketing. Include the mailing address you would like the book sent to.

ISBN: 0-9671253-1-6

Published by:
Lanewood Marketing
11330 Lanewood Circles
Eden Prairie, MN 55344
Phone: (952) 941-7272
Fax: (952) 934-4585
Email: Mary@graduationparty.com
Website: http://www.graduationparty.com

**Attention Schools:**
Lanewood books are available at quantity discounts with bulk purchase for fundraising purposes. For information, please contact Lanewood Marketing.

Have a good graduation party idea? Send it to us!

# Hang on to Your Mortarboards!!!

*Graduation: Celebrate with Style!* will answer all your graduation party questions, including where and when to have your open house, how many invitations to order, what type of food to serve, unique gift ideas, fun suggestions for simple home improvements and exciting extras to make this occasion a very memorable experience. Read on for: to-do-lists, budget worksheets and a down-to-the-wire graduation schedule.

You will also find suggestions on hosting a safe prom party and graduation night "Lock-in Parties."

**Quick Look-up Table (not all subjects are listed here)**

# About the authors

When **Mary J. Anderson's** son Ryan graduated from high school in 1998 she found few, if any, resources available to help her plan his graduation open house. After networking with other parents she discovered a wide variety of resources and hosted a memorable celebration. She was also invited to many graduation parties. Since then she has interviewed over fifty parents about their graduation parties, met with many caterers, event planners, rental companies, restaurant managers, entertainment providers, high school administrators and invitation printers.

She speaks at community education programs and offers lively interviews with the media, Mary is now known as "The Grad Lady." With her daughter Ashley approaching her own graduation you can bet that party will be fantastic.

**Ginger Venable** is an event planner, writer and marketing professional who loves to host a party! As the mother of three, she has had plenty of experience entertaining large groups of kids and grown up kids alike.

Mary and Ginger are certain that this book will provide inspiration and creative ideas to any parent planning a graduation party, prom party or graduation night lock-in. They wish you a fabulous graduation celebration!

Have a good graduation party idea? Send it to us!

# Acknowledgments

Thank you to our family and friends who helped us in so many ways. Special thanks to the parents, children and professionals who allowed us to interview them for this book. We appreciate your great ideas!

Celebrate!!

Ginger Venable & Mary J. Anderson

The Anderson Family, 1998

*This book is dedicated to:*
*Ryan Anderson, Nick Anderson (deceased),*
*Ashley Anderson,*
*Scott Venable, Jackie Venable and Charlie Venable*

# The Calm Before The Storm

Whether this is your first child graduating from high school or your last, the excitement involved in a senior year will astound you. You will be overwhelmed by the number of activities that your graduate will be invited to participate in. You will be confused by all of the choices you have to make concerning post-high school education. And you will be wrapped up in the excitement of celebrating everything from your child's last "first day of school", last football game, prom, and of course the big event itself, graduation!

*Input for this guide was received from over forty parents, graduation experts, party planners, caterers and graduates. It is our goal to offer you the best options and advice we could pull together for planning a graduation party. So the advice comes from a variety of different characters, and will hopefully inspire you to be creative and imaginative.*

## GRADUATION OPEN HOUSE

There never seems to be enough time to plan. But don't worry. This book is going to help you get to work, make your life easier and help you plan a special party for your graduate. This book is going to prevent you from getting to that panic stage (and avoid some of the mistakes some of us have made.)

Have a good graduation party idea? Send it to us!

## DO WHAT YOU DO BEST!

Think about what you do well. If you and your graduate really like entertainment, focus on that. People will remember a live band more than your potato salad. If cooking is your forte, concentrate on a menu that includes some memorable items. If decorating and fun games turn you on, go for it!

## PROM PARTIES

Hosting a before prom or after prom party in your home is a great opportunity for you to get involved in your graduate's celebration and to spend time with their friends. Whether they are going to share the evening with lots of friends or go with just their date we offer some fun alcohol-free suggestions.

## GRADUATION LOCK-IN PARTIES

We have also included some advice on parties hosted by the school and organized by the parents. As concern rises concerning drinking and driving, graduation lock-in parties have become more and more popular. In this section you will find ideas for your school function. Getting involved on this parent volunteer opportunity provides one last chance to meet and get to know the parents of other seniors. Do It!

# Don't Forget the Guest of Honor!

Let's stop and think. Who are you doing this for? Hopefully your interest in planning a graduation party is to celebrate this major milestone in your son or daughter's life. Your graduate will look back on this time as possibly the happiest time in their life (or they may just be glad they survived the torture of puberty). Either way, from now on your graduate will classify their experiences as *before* high school graduation versus the rest of their life.

Since graduation is a monumental experience for your graduate, make them the center of attention — the Guest of Honor.

If you loose sight of this as you plan for *their* party, you may find yourself screaming "you never appreciate the things I do for you!" Let your graduate make choices right up front. Begin by asking them:

> *"What kind of graduation celebration do you have in mind?"*
>
> *"Shall we invite just our close relatives and a few friends, or do you want a huge party?"*
>
> *"Would you like to have a joint party with a friend or neighbor?"*
>
> *"Do you have any ideas for a theme?"*
>
> *"What kind of food would you like to serve?"*
>
> *"Would you like to select photos and items to display?"*

**Have a good graduation party idea? Send it to us!**

As you progress with your party plans, be sure to keep them involved in the decision making process.

Let them help select or make the invitation and the invitation list.

Help them schedule their time for attending other graduation parties and school events.

Select items to display that put your graduate in a good light. They may be funny, but don't put out photos they don't like.

Write them a nice letter before the big day. We have a short sample letter that may help you get started. See appendix.

Always remember this is their graduation. Help them celebrate!

## Lobby Your Graduate for a Party!

*Some kids don't want any type of party at all. We suggest you encourage them to have some kind of celebration, especially if they are just feeling unsure of themselves. Bringing all of the graduate's family and friends together for a celebration of their accomplishments can do wonders for a person's self-confidence.*

*So lobby for a party if your graduate seems ambivalent.*

*Mary's son didn't want a party at first, but after he started hearing about all his friends' parties, then he changed his mind.*

*But if they really don't want to make it happen, let yourself off the hook and plan a special dinner. Do not take on planning a big party if your graduate is not interested.*

# What Kind of Party Fits Your Graduate?

Your first job is to decide what type of party do you and your graduate want to have. There are many options: an open house with a few people, an open house with a hundred people, a party in the daytime, a party in the evening, a celebration on the week-end or during the week. You can have it on a boat, on a beach, in a hall or restaurant or even on a train.

**DARE TO BE DIFFERENT**
You need not spend an arm and a leg to create an interesting and memorable event. Whether you are striving for an exciting gala with dancing and laughter or a quieter, more dignified event, take the time to plan ahead and be creative.

One non-traditional approach is to throw a party for a group of friends graduating together. Does your graduate have friends or relatives who are also graduating? Perhaps two or three families could go in together and host one large get together. Joint parties take some coordinating, but sharing in the shopping, food preparation and expenses will likely be worth the strategizing.

If there is any one single message we want to emphasize, let your party reflect your graduate and dare to be different. Whatever you do, don't feel compelled to keep up with the your friends and neighbors or the Jones's. Again, it's your

Have a good graduation party idea? Send it to us!

graduate's party. Create an event they will remember fondly. What do they want?

Read on for suggestions on locations, themes, decorating ideas, invitations and the menu.

## Make Your Own Kind of Music

*A unique party idea will leave a lasting impression on your graduate as well as your guests.*

*Kathy says: "When we planned our second son's graduation party we wanted to do something different, so we hired a live band, served snacks and pop. The kids loved it!"*

*Maureen organized a dinner cruise for her daughter and her two cousins that were all graduating from different schools. Sharing the expenses with family made it feasible and it was very convenient for all of the relatives to come to one special event!*

# Your Red Letter Day

Picking a date is your first major commitment. Look at the calendar. What works best for your family? Your relatives? Are there any events already scheduled? (In our town the graduates celebrate with a "lock- in" all night party immediately following the ceremony.) Are some of your out-of-town guests going to want to bring their school-age children? When does school get out for them?

Warning... Weekends in June are very busy. First of all, a lot of people will be having graduation parties on the same weekend as the graduation ceremony. *In fact this is one of the reasons we decided to write this guide. We want to encourage parents to spread out their graduation parties. So we can all attend more parties!*

There will be several events that you may not even be aware of that may conflict with your date. For example, the end of the year school team/club banquets are usually not scheduled far ahead of time. Check the school district calendar first, and call your coaches and teacher advisors for information on "unscheduled" events. Area churches may organize a Baccalaureate service (a nondenominational service). And, of course, in the month of June, there are also weddings competing for your guests' time, as well as that of the rental and catering services.

Have a good graduation party idea? Send it to us!

Be sure to check with neighbors. You don't want to have an open house at the same time if you're both inviting enough people to fill a stadium. Parking could be a problem.

When you think about the date, decide if you would like to celebrate in the morning, the middle of the day, or the evening. Again we encourage you to be different.

As soon as you've picked your date, let out-of-town family and friends know so they can plan a trip. A postcard or phone call will do. You will probably follow up with a formal invitation closer to the date.

*"We strongly recommend having your party before the graduation. People are excited to attend the open houses, and are not exhausted from going to so many. You also have a much better chance with caterers and rental companies if you plan a celebration in May instead of June. However, look out for Memorial Day and our favorite, Mother's Day. The parties that are held in May, before Memorial Day, usually get the best turn-out."*

Side note: Think twice about planning any optional trips around this time. You don't want to miss out on other fun parties and activities.

# Location, Location, Location

Maybe you are thinking: "I don't know if our house is really the right place to have this party." If so, you might want to think of some other options.

Here are some alternative locations:

- ❏ Parks: City parks have pavilions that can be reserved for group events. Call your city offices for more information. Some parks charge an entrance fee. Your graduate's friends may not be willing to pay. Perhaps you can make arrangements with the park so that your guests do not have to pay.
- ❏ Health Clubs (which usually have party or rec rooms)
- ❏ Country Clubs
- ❏ Apartment Complex Party Rooms: Do you or someone you know live in an apartment complex that has a party room available to their residents? There are usually fees associated with renting the room.

- ❏ Restaurants (private rooms are available at a variety of restaurants)
- ❏ Hotels: When selecting a hotel, consider what special amenities they may have for your guests who may choose to stay in the hotel. For example, Ginger's Aunt Sheri selected a hotel with a large pool and play area for the guests to enjoy before and after the party.
- ❏ Churches

**Have a good graduation party idea? Send it to us!**

- ❏ Community Activity Centers
- ❏ Cul 'de sacs
- ❏ Airport Hangers
- ❏ Swimming Pool
- ❏ Banquet Facilities
- ❏ Ski Chalets (may be available for rent in the off-season).
- ❏ Bowling Lanes (may have party rooms).
- ❏ Resorts in your area
- ❏ Boats, Yachts, Charter boats.

If you are looking for a unique location, contact a few local caterers for their suggestions. They will be familiar with a variety of potential party sites.

Again, you might want to combine your party with another graduate. If you share the expenses associated with renting an alternative facility, you will avoid the expenses associated with getting your house ready.

If you have the party at a lake or swimming pool, you may want to consider hiring a lifeguard. It will give you peace of mind especially if there are little kids in the pool.

# Making Memories, Choosing a Theme

If you really want to do something different, something that will be remembered, we suggest a theme party.

- **Bon Voyage:** Is your child moving out? That's an added reason to celebrate! Hang bon voyage signs!

- **Thank You:** Invite all of your graduate's teachers, coaches, and special friends who helped them along their way.

- **Off to College:** Is your graduate going to college? Deck the walls with college pennants, banners and jerseys from their new school. Check out their web sites. Many colleges sell merchandise over the internet.

Here is a wonderful way to help your graduate keep in touch with their friends who are going off to college: Buy a large map of the United States and supply pins with labels for the kids to write their names on them. Ask them to print their names and the names of their colleges on the label and put the pin on the map. It is a great conversation starter for the older guests as well.

Does your graduate's future college lend itself to an even more specific theme party? Texas BBQ? Florida Beaches? Boston Seafood?

- **Jock Rock:** Is your son or daughter into sports? Do they love the music played at sporting events? Develop a theme around their favorite sports. Hang all their old jerseys on clothes lines around the yard, or in the house. (The little ones are real cute). Buy all of the Jock Rock CDs (a collection of music played at professional sports events) and play them during the party!

Have a good graduation party idea? Send it to us!

**Class Clown:** Has your graduate always been a fun loving kid? Celebrate this uniqueness with an inspirational focus on humor. Ask your guests to think of funny stories and roast the graduate. Make a poster of silly photos. Hire a comedian to write and perform a funny tribute.

- **Mexico:** Did your graduate study Spanish? Did they go to Mexico? Decorating is easy for a Mexican theme, and who can resist a taco bar? Borrow a sombrero, rugs and wall hangings and display your memorabilia with it. Consider inviting your student's language teachers.

  - **France:** Did your graduate study French? Oui? Ooh la la, build on that theme. French bread, exotic cheeses, French pastries set-up around the French flag or a miniature Eiffel Tower.

  - **European:** Is your graduate going to back pack through Europe this summer? Decorate with travel posters, and your invitation could be a passport.

- **Traveling Man:** Is your graduate taking a road trip to see America the beautiful? Ask your guests to recommend a destination by marking a spot on a map of the US. Maybe they have friends or relatives your graduate can visit. Hang travel posters that you can get from travel agencies. We even saw a miniature hot air balloon at one party!

- **Backyard Brunch:** Is breakfast their favorite meal? See our fun food section.

- **Dance:** Does she love to dance? Splurge on a band or DJ and let music take center stage. Just serve snacks and soft drinks.

- **Member of a Band?** Have a backyard concert, and send out tickets for invitations.

- **School Spirit!** Really emphasize the school your child is graduating from by decorating with the school colors, logo and team jerseys.

- **Beach Party!** If you can't get to a real beach or lake, fill up a plastic kiddie pool with ice and arrange your salads and other perishable food to keep them cool throughout the party. Serve beverages with cute straws and little umbrellas. Have plenty of beach balls, yard games, patio umbrellas, lawn chairs and beach towels.

- **New York, New York:** Is your graduate heading to Broadway? Decorate with signs that look like movie theatre signs and lights. Make your invitation in the form of a theatre ticket.

- **Drama Party:** Was your graduate involved in the school plays? Maybe you could borrow props from the school and invite a few friends to dress up and perform for the crowd.

- **Private Showing:** Is your graduate an artist? A photographer? Have a showing of their work. (Did you know you can rent easels from party rental companies?) This theme lends itself to a great invitation!

**Have a good graduation party idea? Send it to us!**

- **Hawaiian Theme**: Was a family trip to Hawaii fantastic? Why not relive those memories and make some new ones. Serve Hawaiian chicken, fancy drinks in coconut shells with pineapple and other exotic fruits. Let Tiki torches set the mood!

- **Sundaes on Saturday:** Cute invitation idea that makes for a simple menu. Just buy big tubs of ice cream and set up a sundae bar.

- **Texas or Southwest:** Decorate with bandanas, red chili pepper lights, and howling coyotes. Serve southwest food or BBQ, corn bread, chips with guacamole and salsa.

- **Friends:** Co-host a party with a few other families and emphasize the friendships in the invitations and memorabilia. Plan a "keep in touch activity" for all the graduates who attend. Offer to produce a "directory" that will list their addresses, phone numbers, e-mail addresses and other pertinent information. Give graduates a postcard addressed to you so they can write when they have their address, etc. Hire a professional photographer to come to the party for a group shot of all of the graduating friends.

# Invitations

There are a lot of resources available for printing invitations. You can order through your school's resource, custom printers or photographers. Many people go with store-bought or the more personalized, do-it-yourself options.

## SCHOOL RESOURCES

There are several companies that cater to the graduation party invitation market. You may have already received an offer through your school. If you've already ordered those, you can always add a more personalized insert.

## CUSTOM PRINTERS

Printers that offer wedding invitations also offer graduation party invitations. Check your local yellow pages for listing under printers. Prices vary widely based on quality of paper, type of printing, use of colors, images, etc.

**Warning**
*If you want to include a senior photo in your invitation, you can order invitations from your photographer.*

*You can not just take a picture, put it on a piece of cardboard, add your party information and take it to the copy store. The copy store will require a written waiver from the photographer.*

*A 1976 law prohibits copying professionally created photographs. So call your photographer to obtain a one-time copyright waiver for a small amount of money. Then you can design your invitation and bring the waiver with you to the printer.*

Have a good graduation party idea? Send it to us!

## PHOTOGRAPHERS

If you loved your graduate's senior photograph, consider ordering your invitations through the photographer. They often offer printed invitations that incorporate photos. Many offer this additional service when you have your photograph taken. Their prices may be high, but the quality of the image will be superior to copying your own photos.

## STORE-BOUGHT

There is also the option of purchasing preprinted invitations at your local stationery store, paper/party supply store, or mass merchandiser, Target, etc. The selection is getting better every year.

## DO-IT-YOURSELF

If you prefer to do something more creative yourself, the sky's the limit. There are some great Clip Art packages available on CD ROM. Check out your local software retailers or order on the internet. They often contain 1,000s of images, so you can use it for lots of other things as well. A great source for graphics, especially for theme parties is the internet. Check out web sites that relate to your theme, or school and pick up the art work. When you find something you want right click on it, select "save picture as" and save it. Be sure to save it in a file you will remember. If you are not a computer wiz, use stickers.

**Some graphic ideas:** hats and tassels, school logo, future college logo, confetti, diploma scroll, baby pictures, graduation photos.

A simple flyer typed up on your home computer costs approximate 5¢ per copy. These can be folded and mailed "as is" or inserted into envelopes.

Adding color adds excitement but increases your price. You can produce a color invitation on a color printer and copy it in color (the lowest price we've found for color copying is 49¢ each). Or buy colored paper and load it into a regular copying machine. Check out your office supply store for some great selections of paper and shop around for copying services. Approximate cost: 10¢ per copy up to 50¢ per copy, depending on paper.

**Thank you cards:** While you are at it, you may want to order your thank you cards and personalized return address labels at the same time to save yourself the trip after the party.

*These attractive return address labels (this image doesn't do it justice, they are metallic!) were purchased through an announcement printer*

Have a good graduation party idea? Send it to us!

# Invitation Samples

The graduation invitation has come a long way since the little cards we sent when we were teens. Since a picture is worth a thousand words, we have included some samples.

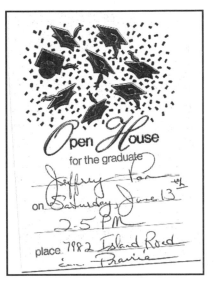

*Traditional announcements are customized for your school. They are classy and formal. Your school will usually offer these sometime during the senior year. They include a formal announcement on the inside. You can personalize your announcement with name cards.*

*Simple invitations to your open house are also offered through your school. You just fill in the student's name, date, time and the location. These are often mailed with the announcement.*

*This attractive photo card (at right) was ordered through a professional photographer.*

Eden Prairie High School
Class of 20XX

*Kelsey Ryan Buell*

**GRADUATION OPEN HOUSE**
17604 Lorence Way
Eden Prairie
Sunday, June 14, 20XX
1:00 - 4:00 PM

*This festive invitation included a clever poem.*

The Tassel was worth the Hassle

It started in kindergarten
She left on the bus
We hoped she'd learn alot
But - Not to cuss

She learned to cross her t's
And to dot her i's
Also, about the birds and bees
That fly in the skies

As the years went by
We grew more and more proud
She certainly proved
To stand out from the crowd

She's accomplished alot
In the past thirteen years
Has loads of ideas
And not many fears

We're having an open house
Please try to save the date
To honor Heather's graduation
In June of

Saturday, June 20    2-6 p.m.    Jackson Drive

Cindy and Buzz

EPHS '98

**CELEBRATE**
Open House for
RYAN B. ANDERSON
Saturday June 13
2-6 p.m.
The Andersons
11330 Lanewood Circle

*This handsome photo card (Mary's son Ryan) was ordered through a professional printer with paid approval from the photographer.*

**Have a good graduation party idea? Send it to us!**

# Funny Invitations

*Here is our favorite funny invitation. It was created on the computer and printed in full color, and folded into quarters.*

...but I'd prefer
that you come to mine!

Justin Wild's Party
Saturday, June 13th
2-5 p.m.

Hosted by the Wild Family
2266 Topview Road
Eden Prairie

943-2266

An Honor Student
is having
a Graduation party!

*This mocked up magazine cover was created by Zach Wigles' parents in full color and printed at home on their color printer. The back side included the party details.*

# Creative Use of Old Photos!

## Our Little Girl...

### Katie

## Is Graduating!!!

**Eden Prairie High School**
**Class of 20XX**

*This creative use of a baby picture with the family rocking chair is charming. Printed front and back on card stock, black only.*

You've Come A Long

Way Baby!

Come Celebrate With Us

*Shayna Graduated*

**Open House**
June 19th,
Noon till 3 PM
8811 Flesher Circle

*This 5 1/2" x 4 1/4" invite was printed in color on card stock.*

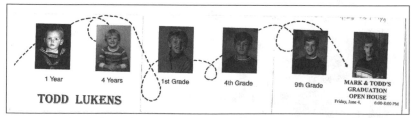

1 Year    4 Years    1st Grade    4th Grade    9th Grade

**MARK & TODD'S
GRADUATION
OPEN HOUSE**
Friday, June 4,    6:00-8:00 PM

**TODD LUKENS**

*This 17" x 4 1/4" long invitation had photos from 1 year old on up to graduation.*

**Have a good graduation party idea? Send it to us!**

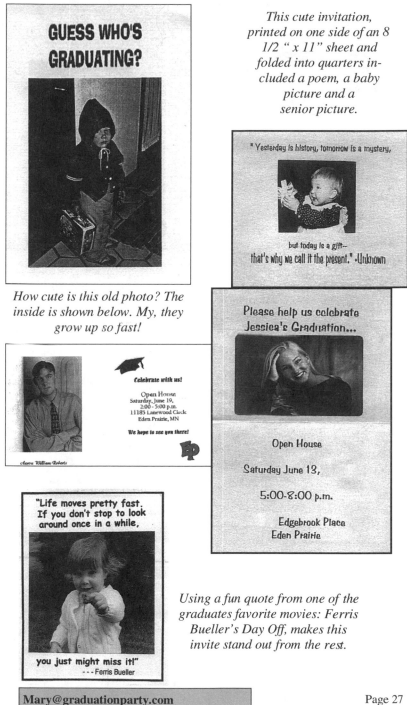

**GUESS WHO'S GRADUATING?**

*This cute invitation, printed on one side of an 8 1/2 " x 11" sheet and folded into quarters included a poem, a baby picture and a senior picture.*

" Yesterday is history, tomorrow is a mystery,

but today is a gift--
that's why we call it the present." -Unknown

*How cute is this old photo? The inside is shown below. My, they grow up so fast!*

**Celebrate with us!**

Open House
Saturday, June 19,
2:00 - 5:00 p.m.
11185 Lanewood Circle
Eden Prairie, MN

*We hope to see you there!*

Aaron William Roberts

Please help us celebrate
Jessica's Graduation...

Open House

Saturday June 13,

5:00-8:00 p.m.

Edgebrook Place
Eden Prairie

**"Life moves pretty fast. If you don't stop to look around once in a while,**

**you just might miss it!"**
--- Ferris Bueller

*Using a fun quote from one of the graduates favorite movies: Ferris Bueller's Day Off, makes this invite stand out from the rest.*

# Group Invitations

*Guess who's graduating?*

We've shared some laughs
We've shed some tears
We've learned so much throughout the years
Our friends are forever
Our memories will last
Class of
It's been a blast.

**ANDY & JEFF**

**ARE GRADUATING AND**

**THEY'RE SO EXCITED!!!**

COME CELEBRATE
ON
SAT., JUNE 20,
3:00 P.M. - 7:00 P.M.
-7454 ANTLERS RIDGE
942-7454

DIRECTIONS:
EAST ON PIONEER TRAIL, RT. ON FRANLO, RT. ON MISTY MORNING, RT. ON ANTLERS RIDGE
DRESS: CASUAL

*Noelle Peterson      Kelly Jacobsen      Katie Norman*

*Celebrate with us at our Open House!*

Saturday, June 14,
5:00 pm until 9:00 pm
Homeward Hills Park

*Hope to see you there.*

*Directions:*
South on 169 to Pioneer Trail; Right on Pioneer Trail (County Road 1); Left at stoplight onto Homeward Hills;
Right on Silverwood to 1200 Silverwood Drive.
Dress: casual

**Have a good graduation party idea? Send it to us!**

*These six studs (and their parents) hosted a party at the beach.*

# The Gang's All Here: Who to Invite

How do you decide who to invite? An easy place to start is your Christmas card list. For some of us, this is an opportunity to do some entertaining. Perhaps there are people whom we owe for parties they've thrown. Many of us feel that we have gone to so many graduation parties that now it's our turn to reciprocate, inviting all of our friends, neighbors and relatives to share in this really special event.

If you are on a budget and feel the need to limit your guest list, keep in mind that, unless you are planning entertainment, most people will stay for less than an hour. Most young people do not eat much, and you do not need to pr o-vide expensive food.

Be sure to get your graduate involved in the "who-to-invite" process. In addition to their friends, they may want to invite some of their favorite teachers or coaches from over the years.

Once you've got your invitations in the mail, ask a dependable friend to take photos during the party. Many people complain that they forgot to take photos. Provide your friend with your camera, film and develop the photos yourself.

**Have a good graduation party idea? Send it to us!**

# Out-of-town Guests?

Most people have friends and relatives who live out of town on their potential guest list. We suggest that you invite those you feel close to.

Some people may feel like they are expanding the list to get more gifts, but similar to a wedding, if your out-of-town guests can not come to the party there is no need for them to send a present. It is simply a nice gesture on your part to share the excitement of graduation.

Decide ahead of time if you are going to invite people to stay in your home and who gets first dibs. Contact your first choice ahead of time to invite them, even before you mail an invitation. If you have room in your home and your heart for more, contact the runner up as well. Keep in mind that your graduate is going to have a lot of exciting activities going on, so don't expect them to spend the whole week sitting home with grandma.

Once you have your house guests lined up, don't hesitate to recommend a nearby hotel to other out-of-town guests and provide a phone number for them to make their own reservations. This way polite people will not ask if they can stay at your house, and you'll be prepared to explain that there is no room at your inn.

# Invitation Checklist

❑ Day and Date: Include the day of the week as well as the date.

❑ Exact Times: Be sure you put the exact times that you want the people there. I saw an invitation that had: *11:00 a.m. - ?* With no ending time. Do you really want people to come as late as 9:00 at night? Do yourself a favor, have a beginning and an ending time.

❑ RSVP: Include this if you like, but sorry to say, usually people do not call. Since some people do not know what RSVP means, we recommend that you state: "Please let us know if you can come by..." Provide a date to call by and your phone number. It's a very busy time of the year and people may say yes and then something comes up. It is frustrating, but you just have to estimate. If you invite 100 people, expect 60 to come.

❑ Location: Give your full address (including city) if you are hosting the party at your home. If you are hosting the party somewhere else, be very specific, i.e. Lake Ann Park Rec Center, 123 Lake Ann Parkway, (North side of lake).

❑ Directions: Provide both a map and written directions, making sure to include your home phone number or the phone number of the location, in case people get lost.

❑ Hosts: If you are sharing the expenses with someone else it is appropriate to acknowledge the other people by name. If it is a joint party, listing the other parents involved helps people identify them.

Have a good graduation party idea? Send it to us!

❏ Full Names: Be sure to use the name your child likes to be known by. Some people like to give personalized gifts and will use the name listed on the invitation, so don't write Charles if your son prefers Charlie.

❏ Dress: If you are throwing an unusual party, be sure to help your guests by specifying this. For example, if you are having a picnic outside say "casual picnic clothes," so women will avoid high heels. If you are out on the lake, state: "Swim suits appropriate," or "We will be swimming."

❏ Gift Suggestions: Unless you're thinking of saying "No gifts please," it is not appropriate to offer suggestions. However, you may want to have a few ideas in case someone calls to ask.

❏ Return Address Labels: If you don't have a large supply of return address labels, you might want to order some custom return address labels. We've seen some with the mortarboard and tassel or confetti that would also be cute for return address labels for your graduate's Thank You cards.

---

**Over Order!**
*There is a tradition that has developed over the last few years that would make Emily Post roll over in her grave. A few weeks before the party, your graduate will want to hand out invitations at school. You save on postage, but give up control of knowing who is invited.*

*Groups of kids will come, travelling around to different parties in packs. Rest assured they don't eat much, they usually don't stay long and are typically on their best "grandma's here behavior." Note: they like cans of pop or bottled water. So, depending on how outgoing your graduate is, be sure to over print your invitations, or you could just make less expensive flyers for your student to hand out.*

# How to Handle Invitations to Other People's Parties

Chances are you and your graduate will be invited to someone else's graduation party. We thought you might appreciate a little advice on this front.

Start a basket to collect all your invitations and encourage

your graduate to put in the ones they receive. Make sure you note which parties you're invited to and which are for your graduate only.

Get a huge calendar and record all the parties you hope to attend. Include the times, in case parties overlap. If there was ever a time to practice good scheduling habits this is the time. Help your graduate keep track of all of their activities, perhaps on their own calendar.

If you are invited to parties on the same day as your own, the odds are you probably won't make it, so if they have requested an RSVP, please call right away, explain the situation, compare notes and offer your congratulations. Keep in mind that you can go to other parties on other days.

Sometimes it gets a little tricky. Are your kids invited? Are you invited? Is the whole family invited? If the invitation is

Have a good graduation party idea? Send it to us!

addressed to the whole family, for example "The Anderson Family," then for sure you're all invited. Sometimes your kids will bring invitations home from school (see Over Order! TIP); my guess is that these are intended as student *only invitations*. If it is someone you know very well, have your graduate ask if you are invited too.

Are you unsure whether or not to bring your younger chi l-dren to an open house? It might be best to hire a sitter. If you know that the family has kids in the same age range, it's usually okay to bring yours. When in doubt, call and ask about bringing your younger children.

**Gift Giving: See the section on gift giving in this book.**

Buy your graduation cards early, they sell out or the selection gets very limited!

# That's Entertainment

If you really want your party to be special, hiring entertainment can make a huge impact. Here is a list of ideas you may want to consider:

- **Caricaturist:** What a fun gift for all of your graduate's fellow students, family and friends. This is very popular with the kids.

- **Handwriting Analyst:** Offers an intriguing look at your personality.

- **Clown:** Yuck it up with some pranks.

- **D.J.:** Dance the night away to a preselected list of your graduate's favorites.

- **Musicians:** Live bands are extremely popular with the graduates. If rock n' roll is not your graduate's style, how about a Jazz Trio, a Pianist, Harpist or vocalists?

- **Face painter:** School logos, shooting stars, or symbols from school activities would be popular for the students (and your smaller guests would love it too).

- **Magician:** Choose either a stage show or strolling performer to compliment "The Magic of Life" theme.

- **Palm Reader or Fortune Teller:** Foreseeing the future is every graduate's wish.

Have a good graduation party idea? Send it to us!

- **Karaoke D.J.:** Are your graduate and friends rock band Wanna-Bes? Make sure you've got some volunteers lined up to get things rolling. It only takes a couple of people to break the ice and the guests will be fighting for the microphone.

**Comedian:** Lighten-up the occasion and add laughter to your party with a comedian who can deliver a stand-up act tailor-made for your graduate.

- **Games:** Casino style, sports or carnival games are popular choices. You can rent a dunk tank, electronic basketball, speed pitch, 9-Hole mini golf, golf challenge, soccer challenge, volleyball, croquet, Bocce ball, or horse shoes. Everyone loves to be a winner. Or how about a moon walk?

- **Photographer–videographer:** Capture this special event with the help of a professional who can stroll the party and ask the guests to pose with your graduate. The videographer can also solicit advice to the graduate.

- **Ventriloquist**

- **Hypnotist**

- **Dancer**

- **Juggler**

- **Hot tub**

# Pay Tribute to Your Graduate

Honoring your graduate is the most important component of the graduation party. If you have been very organized over the years, you probably have all of your photo albums up to date. But if you're like us, family photos are in boxes and piles all over the house. Now is the time

 to start organizing your pictures. Our personal opinion is that you don't want to over do it. Granted, some graduates have an abundance of awards and trophies, but pick and choose what really represents your graduate. Whether it's academic achievements, sports or music, display their photos, trophies, awards and clippings from the paper in an exciting way.

Some people do one big "shrine" while others spread things around. Either way, it's nice for people to see all of the things that your graduate has accomplished.

## Include Friends in Displays and Scrapbooks

*Don't limit the pictures to just your son or daughter. Include photos of the graduate with their friends, extended family and "teams." Your guests will get a kick out of seeing themselves throughout the years. As a keepsake for your child, a photo display that includes other people, not just themselves, is more meaningful.*

Have a good graduation party idea? Send it to us!

**Poster boards:** Some people put photos and news clippings on poster boards propped up on easels (which can be rented). Dress it up with their name, stars, stickers and cut out decorations. Include photo captions if the picture is unclear or you need to identify other people in the picture. Your guests will love to see themselves and their names on the board with your graduate.

**Video:** You may want to think about a video. A continuously playing "video biography" of your son or daughter from birth through high school set to music is an excellent why to share the memories at a graduation party.

You and your graduate could create one together, using your own VCR; or, if you choose, professional services are available. Enlist your child's help in selecting photos and music. Videos make a great keepsake and special gift for your child.

One of our friends later used the video at her daughter's wedding, after adding new footage from the groom's side of the family.

**Display their artwork:** Select a few of your favorites and have them framed or mounted on display boards. Your guests will enjoy seeing the guest of honor's work and the graduate can keep the framed pieces forever.

**Photo Albums:** People love looking at photo albums, especially the new custom creative scrap book type. Its worth the effort to pull together photos of your graduate and their friends, teams and special memorabilia. Assemble a few select photos per event and design a page that identifies who is in the photos, the occasion and any other special information. An album makes a great gift for your graduate after the party. Or have your son or daughter put together the book they want.

Cropping workshops are a great place to get caught up on your album projects, get inspiration, new ideas and get away from the distractions of home. Workshops are offered in homes or at scrap book supply stores. Organize a scrap book party with or without your graduates. If you feel overwhelmed, there are people who organize scrap books professionally. So check with friends or stores that cater to this type of scrap book.

Have a good graduation party idea? Send it to us!

Don't forget to leave room in your album for your graduation pictures.

## Other Photo Display Ideas:

If all else fails, buy one of those display boxes that simply requires stacks of photos or gather existing family albums.

Our friend Beth bought one of those new photo screens and had photos of her daughter Abby blown up to fit the frames. It's an elegant piece of art to keep forever.

If you have any extra photos, we suggest taping them to the underside of your glass top patio furniture, or mounting them on your picnic table with clear contact paper.

## Display Their Pin or Button Collection

If your graduate has been collecting pins and buttons throughout school, find a throw pillow, or favorite jersey and pin all of the pins on it. It's also a great item to find in their room when they come home to visit or to display in their dorm room at college.

## Make Your Tribute Public

Consider buying a congratulations ad in your local paper.

# Deck the Halls, Walls and Doorways

Here is a chance to get really creative and have some fun.
Here are a few ideas:

❑ Banners with "Congratulations Graduate" and the year. Personalized banners can be ordered.

❑ Streamers and crepe paper in your graduate's high school or college colors or choose your own color theme.

❑ Balloons, balloon bouquets, or balloon arches. Be sure to order your balloons ahead of time, especially if you want a lot. The selection of graduation balloons is incredible, so go in to the store and select them ahead of time. Most stores require prepayment for large orders. Some stores will even deliver!

❑ Hang your graduate's graduation gown, mortar board and tassel.

❑ Flowers or candles in your graduate's school colors.

❑ Buy some large inexpensive vases in the school colors. One mother we interviewed reused the vases and created unique arrangements for all three of her children's graduation parties. For her son's she used sports memorabilia instead of flowers.

❑ Hang old jerseys and uniforms on a clothes line. (The little ones, if you still have them, are really cute. )

❑ We went to a party that was for three girls who were going off to different schools. They had pictures of each girl's face attached to the sweatshirts from the different schools, Iowa State, St Benedicts and Wisconsin.

❑ Shiny ribbons, lace, tinsel, metallic tissue paper tied among balloons or draped over chandeliers are dazzling.

Have a good graduation party idea? Send it to us!

- Decorate your table top with confetti and little numbers of the year.

- Hang college pennants, jerseys and sweat shirts from the college your graduate will attend.
- Rent neon signs or lit-up marquee-type signs with an appropriate theme.
- If you have a school mascot, can you borrow the costume from the school? Or buy stuffed animals, for example: eagles, cougars, hawks.
- Hang up the want ads and draw big arrows and circle the funny occupations your graduate may pursue.
- Fill your graduate's car or room with balloons.
- Collect and print out famous quotes and advice on education, life, careers, happiness. Mount them on colored tag board and scatter them around the room. (Tip: Use a huge font)
- Did you check out our theme ideas?

**Deck the Yard!**

*Post some signs in your yard with your graduate's name on them. You never know when these may save guests from crashing the wrong party!*

*Mary and her husband were driving to a party for Sean, our son's friend. We saw some balloons and thought, "Oh, here it is," and walked up to the house. But then – oops! The "Congratulations Sarah" sign startled us into realizing that Sean lives next door. Yard signs help guests who don't know exactly where your house is. Attach balloons to the sign to convey a party atmosphere.*

*P.S. Don't be surprised if we crash your party. We are always doing research for the next edition of our book!*

Jackie's Party!

# Ideas for Creating a Personal Touch

- Print up a large poster containing a photo of your graduate and the answers to the most common questions he or she will likely be asked.
  - Where are you going to school?
  - When do you start?
  - What's your major?
  - Where are you working?
  - Where are you living?

  Be sure to include your graduate's name at the top. This "answer-to-your-questions" poster is a good way to start conversations!

- Have your graduate's photo scanned and printed on balloons or posters!

- Spray paint a chair in your graduate's school colors and have guests sign the chair with a permanent marker. It will become a great keepsake.

> **Postcards to your graduate**
>
> *Have several postcards preaddressed to your graduate and ask your guests to write a supportive note to the graduate. Explain that you will hold on to them until they go off to college or have found an apartment. Mail them to your son or daughter sporadically or on an as needed basis after they have moved.*

- Our friend Terry had a guest book for people to write greetings and warm wishes. She included a note "Please write a note to my son, give him some advice or just wish him the best as he goes off to college." You could also hang a decorated tag board for guests to write their greetings.

Have a good graduation party idea? Send it to us!

# Festive Paper Products

It's fun to have your plates, napkins, and cups match your school colors or your decorating theme. Mary purchased too many plates and cups, but she can use them for other parties in the future. We know from experience that such products in your graduate's school colors are going to sell out fast, so shop early for paper goods. Save all of your receipts. Many stores accept returns on unopened packages.

Think ahead. What are your school's colors? Ours are red and black, so when the red napkins go on sale after Christmas or Valentines Day, buy then. Buy extra. Even if you have hundreds left over, you can use them forever. Unlike food they don't spoil.

Holiday's to watch out for – for your paper product needs.

- Halloween for black and orange
- St. Patrick's day for green
- Christmas for green and red
- Hanukkah for blue
- Easter for yellow, pale blue and purple

Just like for weddings you can have napkins imprinted with the graduate's name and the date of his or her graduation.

### Name tags

Have colorful name tags and ask guests to add a line about how they know the graduate.

## Tableware checklist

- ❑ Large plates (if you're serving a buffet, 2 plates per person)
- ❑ Small plates (if you're serving cake, have 1 per person)
- ❑ Napkins (if you're serving a buffet, 2 per person)
- ❑ Cups (hot and cold if necessary, 2 per person)
- ❑ Cutlery (if you're serving a buffet, 2 per person and don't forget extra forks for cake)
- ❑ Toothpicks
- ❑ Tablecovers
- ❑ Serving bowls and trays
- ❑ Ice bucket
- ❑ Chafing dishes
- ❑ Sterno
- ❑ Crock pot
- ❑ Steaming pans
- ❑ Serving spoons or tongs

**Have a good graduation party idea? Send it to us!**

# Setting up a Gift Table

Gifts are an exciting part of the event. Be sure to have a plan for where to put gifts. Select a table, or book shelf that is away from the front door and the main entertaining area. You do not want to look greedy, or make any guests that did not bring a present feel bad. Don't make a sign or anything tacky, just let your graduate and any helpers you've got for the party know where to put gifts.

## Decorate a Secure Card Box

A traditional gift for the graduate is money. We recommend that you make a receptacle for cards. Decorate a shoe box and cut a large hole in the top for cards to be slipped into. How about using a bird cage or decorating a mail box? Get creative, but be sure to place it away from the door and consider taping it to the table so no one is tempted to walk off with it.

## Opening Gifts

It is not customary to open gifts in front of the guests. Most people do it after the guests have left, or the next day. But sometimes one of your guests asks the graduate to open their gift (maybe they want to see his or her reaction). Your graduate should open the gift and express their gratitude (or laugh as the case may be). But they shouldn't open other gifts.

# Food for Thought: Planning the Menu

Once again, consult your graduate. If you've agreed on a theme, be sure to maximize the opportunity to find foods that fit the theme.

We encourage you to be imaginative! For example, if your graduate is a pizza freak, serve pizza. It is an unusual open house item, and yet the number one most popular food amongst teenagers. You can even have gourmet pizza's.

If your graduate loves desserts, have a dessert party that starts at 7:00 p.m., and specify "dessert party" on your invitation so people know to eat dinner earlier. Desserts can be made ahead and require little serving time. The bakery is an easy way out.

## Quantities?

*If your open house is on a day with dozens of other get-togethers, people may not be very hungry, after attending so many parties. However, relatives, friends, and neighbors attending just your party will eat more.*

*Parents of graduates will be on the go, sampling delights at many parties. So review your invitation list with this in mind.*

*Kids are not going to eat that much.*

*Also, it's ok to run out of food. You don't have to feed the world. Just put away the serving dish that is empty.*

Have a good graduation party idea? Send it to us!

# Creative Food Ideas

### Brunch ideas:

- Take the simple and in vogue route and offer a variety of fresh baked bagels and a big selection of spreads.

- Cook pancakes on a big griddle and serve them with different toppings/syrups.

  - We all love frosted doughnuts! Order ahead for a quick stop at the bakery. You can even request frosting in your school colors. Be sure to have lots of napkins!

  - You can prepare hard boiled eggs with your graduate's name and the year on them and place them in a beautiful basket.

- How about an omelet bar? Make batter ahead of time, and have helpers making custom omelets. Provide shredded cheese, onions, cubed ham, mushrooms, salsa, and green peppers.

  - Coffee bar kiosk: Check with a caterer or the local coffee shop for service or supplies. Or create your own with rental equipment and supplies.

  - Serve exotic juices, or use your juicer to prepare custom beverages.

- Serve fresh fruit in a watermelon boat. Cut your school logo out of the watermelon.

- BBQ sandwiches, ribs or chicken served with cole slaw, baked beans and a fruit salad. Tip from the professional caterer for the BBQ: If you want to use the grill, reduce your stress and precook your meat.

- Italian pasta bar: Add grilled vegetables and salad for a great combination.

- Mexican taco bar: Serve spicy  ground beef in a crock pot, and put the cold items (lettuce, tomatoes, cheese, salsa, olives, onions) in bowls floating on ice to keep them cool. Arrange the taco shells in a Mexican serving bowl or basket.

- Buy large bread shaped like the graduation year. Serve it with spinach dip or do a big submarine sandwich. Plan ahead on how you are going to keep the hoagie cool while it sits out for several hours. We recommend setting it on ice. Rectangle shaped  flower pots can be bought in various sizes. Or a wallpaper hanging trough will do the job.

- Hoagie or Sandwich Bar: let your guests assemble their own sandwiches. Stop by your local submarine sandwich shop for inspiration. Or order a big variety to be sliced and served as needed. Keep the back up in your refrigerator.

- Rent a popcorn machine. It adds a festive  flair and the kids love to serve themselves. Buy extra packages as unused popcorn can be returned.

**Have a good graduation party idea? Send it to us!**

- Shish Kabobs/Skewers
- Salad bar and fresh fruit for the health nuts
- Oriental Food
- Baked Potato Bar
- Gourmet Pizzas
- Swedish Meatballs
- Tortilla Wraps
- Lasagna
- Veggie Tray
- Kiosks: If you've got the space and time to set this up, we heard a cute idea for kiosks, or stations, similar to a carnival or fair. Set each station up in a different part of the room or yard and serve different items at each. For example: hot dogs, pickles on a stick, deli sand-wiches, iced tea, root beer floats.

**Budget TIP!**

*Worried that you might run out of food? Stock up on back-up items like nuts, pretzels, chips and salsa, chicken nuggets, cheese poppers, candy, bottled beverages and cookies.*

*If you are concerned that you will have too much food, plan ahead. Stock up on plastic containers and make room in your freezer. As soon as the party is over freeze as many things as you can or send it home with your friends.*

*Another alternative is to plan ahead to bring the left-overs to a shelter. Some shelters have rigid standards, so call ahead to see what types of dona-tions they accept.*

# Tasty Desserts

- Custom cakes: Have you seen the new  photocake? How about a custom cake made in the shape of a basketball or tennis shoe? Here is your chance to have your cake and eat it too. Order one custom cake to display and a second cake to cut and serve. Save some time and have the cake delivered. Can't decide on what to serve? Order two: carrot cake and white cake.

- Smores at a fire pit. Provide several baskets full of marshmallows, chocolate bars and graham crackers. Have plenty of roasting sticks on hand.

- Cut out your school logo on a watermelon boat. This takes some talent, but it's an inexpensive and special touch.

- Ice cream sundae bar: serve ice cream with different toppings, fruit, cookies, and coffee. Its easy, fun and guests will love it.

- Frozen treats from your favorite ice cream specialty store, packed on dry ice.

- Trays of your graduate's favorite bars, cookies and candy. Or, use a cookie cutter shaped like a graduation mortarboard. If you have family members who like to bake, ask them to help.

- Fortune cookies?

Have a good graduation party idea? Send it to us!

- Custom made chocolates: Order gold foil-wrapped coins with your graduate's name on one side and the year on the other (Custom Chocolate, (651)646-3031.)

- Root beer floats were a huge hit at our friend's party. She offers this time saving tip: Scoop the vanilla ice cream into plastic cups and freeze them overnight. Then at the party all you have to do is add root beer and a straw. You can buy a keg of root beer from the liquor store.

- Cheesecakes in a variety of flavors served with different toppings. For example: hot fudge, strawberries, blueberries.

- We saw this idea for chocolate mortarboards in the Family Fun magazine (great magazine!). Place miniature peanut butter cups, bottom up, on a plate. Top with a small dollop of peanut butter, then press on chocolate covered graham crackers. For a tassel, cut up a long rectangle of fruit roll-ups, keeping part of the little square in tact, cut little tassels. Stick on top of cookie. This is a great project to have younger siblings help with – and they look so cute!

- Buy lots of suckers in your school colors.

# Popular Graduation Party Recipes

Cooking for a large group? Try these grad-pleasing dishes.

## Cheesy Chicken for 50

20 cups diced cooked chicken
10 cups chopped celery
4 bunches chopped green onions
16 ounces chopped green chilies (canned)
2 - 6 ounce cans sliced pitted ripe olives (drained)
4 cups slivered almonds
4 cups mayonnaise
4 cups sour cream
10 cups crushed potato chips
10 cups shredded cheddar cheese

Combine the first eight ingredients with 4 cups of the cheese.
Mix well and spoon into four greased 13" x 9" x 2" deep
baking dishes. Sprinkle with chips and remaining cheese.
Bake, uncovered, at 350° for 25 minutes or until hot.

## Macaroni Salad for 50

3 pounds cooked ham, cubed
3 pounds macaroni, cooked and drained
4 cups shredded cheddar cheese
1 bag frozen peas, thawed
6 cups chopped celery
1 large chopped onion
1 5 3/4 ounce cans pitted sliced ripe olives

**Have a good graduation party idea? Send it to us!**

Macaroni Salad Dressing:
1 quart mayonnaise
4 ounces Western brand salad dressing
1/8 cup vinegar
1/8 cup sugar
1/2 cup light cream
1 teaspoon onion salt
1 teaspoon garlic salt
1 teaspoon salt
1 teaspoon pepper
Make dressing in a separate bowl. Combine all ingredients and pour dressing over salad. Refrigerate.

## Brunch Baked Omelet (3 pans for 40 people)
This recipe is for one pan.

8 pieces of buttered bread (cubed)
3 cups cubed ham or turkey
4 cups shredded Cheddar cheese
6 eggs
3 cups milk
2 tsp. Dry mustard
Salt and pepper

Arrange bread, cheese and ham in buttered 9 x 13 pan. In separate bowl beat eggs, dry mustard, salt, pepper and milk. Pour slowly into pan. Bake at 350° for one hour. Eggs will start to pull away from edges of dish when ready. Let set 5 minutes or so, cut into squares.

# Whet Your Appetite: Beverages

Provide your guests with a variety of beverages to choose from. Here are a few suggestions:

- A summer tradition of big pitchers of iced tea, lemonade or Kool-aid are refreshing.
- If you want to serve soda, most people we interviewed suggest liters instead of cans. It goes a little further, and you don't have half drunk cans all over your house.
- If you do serve cans, put out a couple of recycling bags or boxes. People will hound you if you don't. You can clean up the official recycling bin you got from your garbage company so that it looks more presentable. If you want more than one, borrow your neighbor's.
- Always provide water for your guests who don't like carbonated beverages. Bottled water is very popular with high school seniors, but pretty pitchers with lemons floating in ice water are refreshing and less expensive.
- Borrow or rent tubs for ice. You can put the sodas right on ice. If you use coolers, label them so people don't have to dig around.
- Punch bowls are fun. Make an ice ring using one of the punch ingredients so that as it melts it will not dilute the punch. A bundt pan works well for an ice ring.
- If you serve a keg of root beer and a keg of real beer, be sure to affix signs that cannot be switched by pranksters.
- Toasting the graduate is fun. Prepare something in advance; you can get a book of toasts from the library or come up with something heartfelt on your own.

Have a good graduation party idea? Send it to us!

## A Word on Alcohol

- Do not serve alcohol to any minors.
- We recommend no alcohol at all.


**Ginger's Punch Recipe:** (great fruit taste, without the color to stain your carpet)

Mix together:
  2 cans frozen limeade concentrate
  2 cans frozen lemonade concentrate
  2 cans unsweetened grapefruit juice
  2 cans pineapple juice

Just before serving add:

  3 quarts ginger ale
  3 quarts chopped ice (or better yet, make an ice ring from
                           one of the ingredients)
  1 quart water

# S.O.S. Don't Be Afraid to Ask for Help

Warning! You cannot cook the food, serve drinks, clean up empty glasses, clean up spills, rewind the video, put music on the stereo and still be the congenial host and introduce your friends and neighbors. If you try to do it all, you won't have any fun at all!

A common complaint from parents after a graduation party is "I wish I would have had more help during the party. I was so busy, I didn't have time to talk to anyone!" So we suggest that you recruit someone to help. Here are some tips:

- Do you have a friend who is hosting a graduation party this spring whom you could swap services with? Call her and say "If you help me with our graduation party, I will be more than happy to help you with yours." If possible, recruit a friend who may not know a lot of your guests. Mary was asked to help a friend at her party, but ended up knowing so many of the guests that she was talking all the time and felt bad later.

## Celebrate in style!

Have a good graduation party idea? Send it to us!

- Do you have friends with children graduating next year? Tell them you promise to help them if they'll help you.
- Do you have helpful relatives planning to come? They may be happy to lend a hand.
- If all else fails, hire somebody through a catering service. It's worth every penny!
- Hire someone through an ad in the paper.
- Hire a food server from your favorite restaurant.
- If you have to hire someone, negotiate an hourly wage, and if you are happy with their performance give them a tip.

Ask your helper to come early and give them instructions. Give them a quick tour of the house, including where to put gifts. Make your expectations clear ahead of time.

Don't assume that people will help, just because they said they were coming. Ask them if they will help ahead of time.

Paying for help may seem like a luxury, but you will have a much better time and you won't be so tired afterwards. If you have someone else doing most of the work during the party, it will give you the time and pleasure to greet your guests, reintroduce your graduate if necessary and mingle with your friends.

# Hire a Caterer?

Hiring a caterer is a great alternative to doing all of the work yourself. If you are hosting the party in your own home, feel free to plan on making or buying some of the food and/or beverages yourself. Leave the labor intensive and time sensitive items to the caterer.

There is a wide variety of caterers to choose from. Working with a good caterer is great fun and should make the party much easier for you.

We have taken the time to interview several caterers and offer the following checklist for your interviews.

**Hot Tip!**

*Call caterers early enough to get on their calendars. Their weekends fill up fast so let them know if you are flexible on dates and times. If you have your party on a week night, you will have a bigger selection of caterers and possibly be able to negotiate lower service rates.*

**Have a good graduation party idea? Send it to us!**

# Caterer Checklist

❑ What are their specialties? (Food and beverage) Do they have a printed menu you could review?

❑ If you have a theme for your party, ask the caterer for recommendations to fit the theme.

❑ What serving equipment do they supply? (platters, chaffing dishes, serving spoons, tongs, plates, silverware, glasses, coffee urns, pitchers for beverages)

❑ Do they rent tables, chairs, linens, table skirts, dishes, silverware? If they don't, they may recommend a service.

❑ Do they provide or rent any extras? (Centerpieces, candles, decorations, props, ).

❑ How do they bill? Insist on a written estimate and breakdown of all costs. Ask to see a sample invoice so you know what to expect.

❑ What is their policy for quantities, can you return anything?

❑ How much space do they need to set up and what do you need to provide for them?

❑ Can they provide you with references?

❑ How do they figure portion sizes?

❑ How many people will staff your event?

❑ Does their staff serve beverages?

❑ Is there a separate delivery charge?

❑ Does their staff clean up during and after the party? What is included in this clean-up service?

Many local restaurants provide catering as part of their services. Some options include picking up the food yourself, delivery (hot or cold), delivery with set-up, and delivery with full service staffing.

# Some Stunning Grad Party Examples

## Monday Night Barbecue and Band

One really well planned party Mary attended was hosted by Jean and Bob. They geared their informal party for kids. They had it on a Monday night(!) from 4:00 to 10:00 for two reasons: They wanted to hire a band and found out that the selection was much greater on a Monday, since most bands are booked on the weekends. They wanted a good turnout and knew most people were not busy on Mondays. They had about 90% turnout!

They rented a tent, tables, chairs and a six-foot gas grill. The  ribs, chicken and BBQ beef on a bun were bought precooked and then reheated on the grill so that it looked like it was actually being cooked on the grill. *Mary thought it was at the time.* They served Caesar salad (which they bought in big 5 pound lettuce bags), chips and watermelon.

Popular with the kids was a peanut butter and jelly table. They loved making their own sandwiches on Wonder Bread. It seemed nostalgic.

A huge hit was a bonfire pit where the guests make their own smores. They provided the long skewers and a basket full of marshmallows, graham crackers, and chocolate bars.

Have a good graduation party idea? Send it to us!

They also had a volleyball game set up which the kids really got into.

They also rocked when the band began to play. The hosts' daughter had picked out most of the songs ahead of time, but the band did take a few requests. Again, the kids loved it.

Jessie, the daughter, was very involved in her party. She set up her own memorabilia table, at which she displayed many clippings she had saved over the years. Her friends and their parents delighted at the chance to step back in time.

Because she loved school, and wants to be a teacher, Jessie invited all of her teachers and principals, from kindergarten on. The ones who were able to attend had a great time chatting about bygone days.

**A Very Very Formal Affair**

Imagine: You're greeted at the door by a gentlemen dressed in a tuxedo who directs you to other tuxedo clad servers who offer you a beverage. A well known pianist is playing the baby grand piano to greet the people as they arrive. The food is served on china and silver. After dinner you are directed to a cappuccino bar where another server awaits your custom order. All we could say was WOW!

## New York, New York!

Two girls who were both going to college in New York shared a party and had a New York theme. They combined Broadway and the disco/nightclub scene for a fabulous evening gala. They had little statue of Liberty's as centerpieces, their invitation was a ticket to a play and they played show tunes for the entertainment.

## A Sunny Brunch

We attended a sunny morning brunch for a high school track star. Her parents had assembled a striped tent in the back yard which protected us from the hot sun. The tables were decorated with bright potted flowering plants. Easels displayed a few portraits of the graduate. The brunch was served buffet style: ham, pasta salad, fruit, muffins, coffee cakes. Another

popular and unusual addition was sliced bagels with a variety of spreads in cute little crocks. The custom cake shaped like a track shoe was fun. Our hosts served a variety of fruit juices and coffee (both regular and decaf). Don't forget the coffee condiments.

Have a good graduation party idea? Send it to us!

**Americana Tradition!**

Linda has hosted two graduation open houses and prefers a traditional "Americana" party. Her advice: Get your tent really early. They are all be booked ahead of time. A tent is like weather insurance. Linda put her tent in the back yard, and decorated with the high school colors. She rented a pop-corn popper, which added a festive flair to the day. For her first party she served BBQ on a bun, beans in a chafing dish, and a traditional graduation cake. The second year she served chicken, corn on the cob, potato salad, rolls and butter, chips and dip. The classic picnic added a traditional flair to the day.

**Progressive Party**

Tessa and her best friend of 18 years, Tricia, organized a shared open house on the day of their graduation from Poly High School in Riverside, California. The invitation shows these two energetic cheerleaders in uniform. The unusual twist to their shared party was that they had a progressive open house, starting at 2:00 in the afternoon at Tricia's house with hors d'oeuvres before the ceremony. Then, after the ceremony, the party moved to Tessa's house for a light dinner of sandwiches and an assortment of cold salads. Tessa's mom, Vickie, ordered a custom cake decorated with a frosting illustration of the girls in their cheerleading uniforms. The girls had to leave at 10:00 p.m. to get to their all-night lock in party, but many of the guests stayed until 11:00.

# Gift Ideas

Here are some graduate-tested and approved gift ideas:

- Gift Certificates to book stores, the local mall or a major retailer.

- Books: We suggest something that graduates can treasure over the years: such as poetry, motivational books, a quality dictionary, a leather bound journal. Or how about one of these classics, *Oh the Places You Will Go*, by Dr. Seuss; *Leaving Home Stories*, by Hazel Rochman; *Brave New World*, by Aldous Huxley; *Atlas Shrugged* by Ayn Rand.

- Sweatshirt or T-shirt with college name. Shop the Internet or The College Store. They also sell cups, pennants and socks!

- Personalized items: Put monograms or name and graduation date on flannel blankets, bath towels, coffee mugs, key chains or frames.

- Large bag for dirty clothes, along with a box of detergent and quarters

- Long distance calling cards

- Snake light or flash light

- Personalized luggage tags

- Camera with battery and film or disposable cameras

- Custom made frame, with personalized words around the edge

- A subscription to your hometown newspaper or the graduates favorite magazine.

- Travel iron or small ironing board

**Have a good graduation party idea? Send it to us!**

- Little hammer and screwdriver set: Check out the trendy hardware stores; they have cute versions of the necessities.
- Pen & pencil sets
- Thank you notes, stationery (monogrammed?) and stamps

- Travel alarm clock
- A supply of stamped post cards you have addressed to yourself and other special family members.
- Book ends
- Big storage bins (fill them with plastic plates or Tupperware for snacks in the dorm room)
- Address book: leather bound adds a nice touch. Be sure to write in your own address.
- Photo albums
- Cooler, filled with beach towels, sun screen, can coolers, plastic wear

## Money, Money, Money!

*It's very common to give a graduate money as a congratulations gift. Some people have asked us, "What is the appropriate amount to give a friend who is graduating?" We maintain that it is like any other time that you choose to give money as a gift, it is totally up to you. Any amount will be appreciated. $20.01, $20.02, $20.03 is cute!*

*Buy your cards early, they sell out or the selection gets limited!*

# Larger Gift Ideas

For those really special graduates in your life, you may want to buy something more expensive. Think about organizing a group gift with relatives or neighbors. Here are some suggestions:

- Luggage or a soft sided travel bag
- For young ladies, how about a gift certificate for a massage, facial, haircut, manicure etc.
- Congratulations ad in the paper
- A computer
- TV

- Microwave
- A small refrigerator for the dorm
- Stereo
- Answering machine
- Cell phone or  pager

- Stocks or bonds
- Frequent flyer pass for a trip home from school or for a fun trip before school
- A homemade quilt. We've seen a really neat quilt made with scanned photos. Our friend found a company that can scan photos onto material and a different person to sew the quilt.

- A charm bracelet
- A watch
- Matching bracelets for all your daughter's friends.

Have a good graduation party idea? Send it to us!

# A Funny and Heartfelt Gift Idea

Print up some postcards on your home computer like these:

**Help!**
**Please send me:**
- ❑ Cookies
- ❑ Money
- ❑ Clothes
- ❑ News from home
- ❑ Photos of your kids
- ❑ Address of your son/daughter at college
- ❑ Other_____

_____

Jackie Venable
Middlebrook Hall, Room 1117
University of Minnesota
Minneapolis, MN 55411

Put your home address on most of them so the graduate knows you are there for them in case of emergency. It's a cute way for the graduate to stay in touch.

# Don't Look a Gift Horse in the Mouth (Advice to Give Your Graduate)

*We were reluctant to include this section in our first edition, but we got a lot of compliments on it and found a lot of parents actually made their graduates read it and discuss options. We've also written a letter to be read by the graduate. (see Appendix) Feel free to rewrite it in your own words, including some of your own feelings.*

We suggest you have a conversation with your graduate about proper behavior during their graduation party. Here are a few suggested ground rules for the graduate to discuss ahead of time:

- Say hello to everyone, a nod across a crowded room is not enough for Aunt Lucy.
- If you see someone you don't know, ask us discreetly.
- Circulate amongst all your guests. You'll have plenty of time later to hang out with your friends.
- Decide with your parents before the party how long you're going to stay. They may want you to stay until the last guest leaves or you may arrange to leave at a certain time to attend other parties.
- Be agreeable and a good sport when it comes to picture taking.
  - Smile! (Ginger has devised a secret hand signal that reminds her daughter to smile.)

  - Wear a nice outfit.

**Have a good graduation party idea? Send it to us!**

- Although you usually won't open gifts in front of the guests, sometimes one of your guests will ask you to open their gift (maybe they want to see your reaction). If this happens, open the gift and express your gratitude (or laugh, as the case may be). But do not open other gifts.

- Since many people will give you gifts of money, we suggest you negotiate a settlement with your parents prior to opening presents. Examples include:

  - You can spend half of the money now, but half of the money received shall be put in your bank account.
  - All of the money will be saved for books at college.
  - You can use the money as a down payment on a car.
- You can use the money for new clothes for work.

**Thank You Notes:**

Every gift (including money) must be acknowledged with a thank you note, so save the cards and write down who gave you what as you open the gifts. We suggest that you set a goal of five cards each day. It's best to get them out within six weeks of the party. Tape the checks to a cupboard and only deposit them when the thank you note has been mailed. Always hand-write the thank you notes and hand address the envelopes. Mention the gift specifically in your note and express your appreciation. Avoid making every thank you look like a form letter by adding a personal reference.

# Freshening Up Your Home

If you've decided to have the celebration in your home, this is a good time to look around your house with a very objective eye. Look at your walls, your carpet, your furniture, your deck, your landscaping and anything else that you may want to change or freshen up.

In what part of your home will the party be held? Three things to keep in mind if you have it outside: weather, weather, and weather. June is a very rainy month in many parts of the country. As much as we would like to have the party on a beautiful, sunny day, we have to plan for bad weather. So ask yourself, "Where can I accommodate the most people?" Guests tend to gravitate to the kitchen because that is where the action is. But you can attract your guests by placing all of the food, beverages and memorabilia in the living room, family room or elsewhere. Another choice is the garage. If you could clear it out, it may provide the best party area. Once you've thought through where you plan to entertain, it's time to look around.

Do you need a fresh coat of paint or wall paper? I know we

did. Having a party was a great reason to paint the walls. Nothing drastic. Just a new coat on

**Have a good graduation party idea? Send it to us!**

the living room, kitchen, halls and entry way really freshened it up. One thing we did a whole year in advance was have the outside of the house painted. We knew that we would be entertaining the following year, so we had it painted in the fall, instead of waiting for spring. We saved the interior painting until closer to the open house (it's amazing how quickly the walls get dirty!)

You might consider new carpet. We didn't, but we did have our carpets professionally cleaned. Some people may want to wait until after the party, but I'm glad we chose to have them done in advance.

I also needed to look at our window treatments. Our drapes had been in the house for as long as

### Money Saving Ideas

*If your budget is limited, consider these ideas:*

- *Host the party in a nearby park. No one need even see your house!*
- *Borrow potted flowers from your neighbors.*
- *Paint just the front of the house, rather than the entire thing.*
- *Scrub the walls and just paint the entry way and dining room.*
- *Rent a carpet cleaner and do it yourself*

we had, 18 years! I knew it was time for a change. I looked in many magazines and stores and decided on new window treatments. It really gave the house a fresh new look.

Looking out my windows I saw years of dirt. I decided to spend the extra money to have my windows professionally cleaned, inside and out. It made the house look bright and clean.

Does your deck need some repair work done? Or maybe you need a

whole new deck or patio. The deck builders are very busy in the summer, so it's a good idea to start early. I understand the carpenters get a little hungry in the winter months, so start early and get that deck put up in time for your graduation party.

Planning a party in your home also gives you a reason to look at your landscaping. You may want to pull out some old bushes, trim them or plant new ones. How about some new flowers? Since most graduation parties are held in late spring/early summer, be sure to plant early blooming flowers.

Does your driveway need new black topping, seal coating or repair?

**Have a good graduation party idea? Send it to us!**

## Don't Worry, Be Happy!

We hope we haven't got you too worked up over this subject. Please remember that you don't have to go crazy over home improvements. Maybe some paint, some landscaping or just cleaning the carpets will make you feel better about entertaining in your house. You probably want to get these things done anyway, but knowing that the big party is coming up is a great motivator.

# Helpful Hints from a Rental Company

- Combine parties with neighbors or friends. Rental costs can be shared. Since most items rent for the weekend, it's easy to share tents, tables and chairs.

- Go in for a consultation. Know what you are getting. You don't want to be disappointed when you get something delivered or come to pick something up. Unless you know exactly what you want and you've seen it before, do not order over the phone. Keep in mind that these are used items, so you might get a table or chair that has a scratch in it, maybe a small stain.

- Rent large vases and decorate with bouquets of flowers and plants from the farmers market. You will be impressed by

## TIPS on Renting Tents!

*Renting a tent for an outdoor party is like buying weather insurance. Call early. It's a simple case of supply and demand.*

*Consider renting tent lighting if your party is at night.*

*To protect your guests from a windy rain rent the tent sides.*

*If possible, use the tent as an entrance to your garage or house. As people approach the house they will get a festive party feeling.*

### How Big?

*A 20' x 20' tent is designed for 40 people. A 20' x 30' for 60.*

Have a good graduation party idea? Send it to us!

the low prices and quality.

- When renting table cloths, order extra in case you spill while setting up.

- Rent easels to display photos.

- If you can't afford to rent both a tent and tables and chairs, consider borrowing tables and chairs from your church.

- Rent a popcorn machine. They are fun, and if you run out of everything else, you can still serve popcorn, (You can return the unused popcorn!)

- Compare the cost of renting chaffing dishes to the cost of buying them.

- Upon delivery, count all of the items and do a quick inspection. Note any damages on the delivery receipt to avoid losing your damage deposit.

If you do not want people walking through your house to use the bathroom, consider renting an outdoor sanitation system. Look in the yellow pages under toilets-portable.

# Food Service Equipment for Rent

The following items are available for rent at rental companies:

- Roaster
- Deep Fryer
- Chaffing Dish
- Soup Warmer
- Heat Lamp
- Charcoal Grill
- Propane Grill
- Salad Bar

- Cotton Candy Machine
- Sno Cone Machine
- Hot Dog Roller
- Nacho Cheese Warmer
- Pancake Griddle
- Popcorn Machine
- Frozen Drink Machine
- Large Coffee Maker

Rental companies also rent banquet tables. When renting tables, remember the table cloths and table skirts. Companies rent linens to fit their tables – as well as fun decorations to put on them.

Remember that there is almost always a delivery charge, which includes pick-up, so try to rent everything from the same place.

Have a good graduation party idea? Send it to us!

# Games & Other Fun Stuff for Rent

The following items are also for rent at rental companies:

- Moon Walk
- Dunk Tank
- Electronic Basketball
- Speed Pitch
- Bowling/Golf Game
- 9-Hole Mini Golf
- Golf Challenge
- Soccer Challenge
- Volleyball
- Croquet
- Bocce Ball
- Horse Shoes
- Pink Flamingos
- Bubble Machine
- Fog Machine
- Mirrored Balls
- Strobe and Spot Lights
- Helium Tank

One new rentable item we were particularly impressed with was a two gallon acrylic drink cooler/dispenser. What we like about it is the fact that the ice is isolated in the middle of the tank and the lemonade, or iced tea is on the outside, so it doesn't get watered down as the ice melts. There is a little spigot that dispenses the beverage. It's very attractive.

# Prom– Oh What a Night!

The key to a great prom, (besides having the right date) is to plan ahead. If your student wants to get into the tanning booth or beauty salon, don't wait until the last minute to make appointments.

Does your son need to buy his date a corsage? Find out what color his date's dress is and what she prefers. Make him order it and pick it up.

> **Money saving TIP!**
>
> *Look for a consignment shop or dress rental company. Most women never wear their dress again.*

### Before the Prom Parties

To avoid any drinking and driving, many families plan and host before and after parties for their graduates. Find out if your graduate plans to go with any other couples and ask the other parents to help you plan a special party. If your plans are for an outdoor party, be sure to have a back-up in case of bad weather.

- Before parties might include hors d'oeuvres and fancy non-alcoholic drinks served in your best glassware.

- Be sure to have plenty of film on hand (both still and video) and think about a good spot to take photos.

- In addition to couple shots, take photos of just the girls and just the guys. Often they are more valuable later when peo-ple would rather forget their date, but love their friends.

- Give the kids enough privacy to enjoy themselves, but don't go out for the evening. Going over to the neighbors is a great way to give the kids privacy, but they know you may be home at any minute.

**Have a good graduation party idea? Send it to us!**

## After Prom Parties

We strongly recommend that you help your graduate plan their activities for after the prom. More problems occur after the prom than before. Again, we suggest that you enlist the support of other parents. Here are some party tips:

- Be sure to have a guest list; you don't want the entire class showing up thinking it's an open party.

- Find out how the kids are getting to your party and what time to expect them. Some people even rent a limo bus to pick up their guests from the dance. (In this case have them drop off their cars at your place beforehand).

- Rent their favorite videos, or for something more exciting, a hot tub, or air trampoline. For more ideas, see the entertainment section of this book.

- Have lots of snacks on hand. Order a late night pizza to be delivered before the pizza place closes, or make your own when they return.

- If you have invited the kids to spend the night, have the guests drop off an overnight bag before the prom, establish an ending time to the party. Serve breakfast.

  - Take the car keys away from the kids, until the next morning.

  - Have all of the graduates sign waivers that state "I will not drink alcohol before, during or after the prom." Make the parents sign it too.

- Don't provide them with too much privacy.

- You may want to search the yard to make sure no one has hidden any alcohol. This may seem extreme, but we have heard of kids hiding alcohol.

## Prom– More Fun Suggestions!

• Encourage your son to be creative about asking his date to the prom. Suggest that he tie balloons to her car with a big sign, "Will you go to Prom with me?" Don't forget to tell him to sign his name! Or he might send her flowers with the invitation printed on a card. If he's unsure of her answer, a discreet invitation is probably best.

• If your daughter is going with a group of girls, try to find a hair stylist who will come to your home before the prom and give manicures, pedicures and hair styles. Or just get all the girls to make an appointment at the same salon. To save money, set up your own salon and give each other manicures, etc.

• If possible have your daughter's hair styled several days before to make sure she likes the style and can keep it in place for the night. Lots of hairspray is a must for many styles.

• Encourage your student to go to the prom whether they have a date or not. Today, many students go to the prom without a date. Don't make your son or daughter feel that they have to accept a date with someone incompatible.

• Encourage your student to offer to share expenses with their date.

• Make sure your student is prepared to dance. Offer to spring for lessons if necessary, even if its with you!

• Encourage your student to wear comfortable shoes. Tell them to break-in new shoes around the house for a few hours every night the week before the prom.

Have a good graduation party idea? Send it to us!

## Renting a Limousine

If you are considering renting a limo for the prom, call way in advance. They book up early. If possible go see the limo you plan to rent; don't count on old photos. Ask these questions:

❑ What are their rates and what is included in that rate?
❑ Can they arrange to pick you up and take you to dinner, take you to the dance and pick you up after the prom?
❑ Do they usually get a tip?
❑ What is the maximum capacity and what is a comfortable number of passengers?

If your student is organizing the limo rental, make sure he or she gets the money from their friends who plan to share it up front. Lots of people may say they want to go in on it, but make sure they back it up with cash.

Parents: Make sure no alcohol is available in the limo.

### Money saving TIPS!

*Make plans to share a limo with another group of students who don't mind starting their evening early and are flexible on the return times, especially if you can dine near the prom location. It's expensive to have the limo sitting in the parking lot for hours.*

*Or just rent the limo for one leg of your evening and drop off cars ahead of time for the return trip.*

*Maybe the parents can meet the limo at the dance and go out for a ride while the graduates are at the dance!*

# Graduation Lock-in Parties

To help the graduates celebrate in a safe environment (no drinking and driving), many schools organize an all night party. The party starts shortly after the graduation ceremony, with transportation provided when the destination is far away. The price of these parties ranges from $30 to $100 per graduate, with lots of prizes and items donated by local businesses.

Riverside, California is a strong advocate for all night lock-in parties. In 1996 instead of going to the all night party, three graduates celebrated by party hopping. Their car ran into a pole going 90 miles per hour. Two young women were killed instantly, and the male driver was left paralyzed from the neck down. Alcohol was involved.

The community was shattered by the event, and many parents were inspired to help promote and volunteer at the all night lock-in party. The first few years they hosted an extravagant all night cruise around Catalina Island. Other nearby high schools have been celebrating with a lock-in at Disneyland.

Have a good graduation party idea? Send it to us!

# Suggestions For The All Night Party

Most school parties are organized by a group of parents. Here is some advice from parents we interviewed:

- Recruit parents of juniors, as they will not be so busy with their own celebrations.

- Start planning in November, but keep the enthusiasm building to recruit as many volunteers for the big night.

- Make students sign an alcohol/drug free contract when they sign-up and pay in advance. Give the graduates a wrist band for proof that they paid.

- Hire a security firm (talk to your police liaison).

- Check out your school's liability contract. If it doesn't cover this event, buy additional coverage through them.

- Secure your location way in advance. Suggestions include: the school itself, a shopping mall, recreation center, zoo. The best places come with some entertainment; for example, if you can get into a mall that already has a video arcade, convince the owners to participate by staying open all night and providing "free" tokens all night. Mall restaurants are often willing to provide a limited menu for the night.

- Hire professionals and negotiate a rate that will ensure that they show up for your event and do not expect tips from the graduates: DJ, band, hypnotist, karaoke, comedian, casino dealers with their own equipment, masseuse, manicurist, make-up artists, caricaturist, photographer (who can provide photos that are ready that night), hand writing analysts, or fortune teller.

- Rent high-quality games: sumo wrestling, moon jump, Elastarun, Jacob's ladder, king of the hill, slides, obstacle course, rafts for pools, giant twister, ping pong, pop-a-shot.

- Offer popular food and drinks: coffee, soda, bottled water, pizza, candy, cotton candy, burgers, popcorn.
- Limit the amount of printing. It can get expensive.
- Have a theme: carnival, cruise, Mardi Gras, popular movie, song, futuristic. Check out our party theme ideas in this book.

> **Money saving TIP!**
>
> *Look for a popular radio station that has a van they could drive into the event and have the DJ broadcast live. Let the graduates request music.*

- Provide a secure "coat check" room for the graduates to stash their coats, bags and prizes they win.
- Organize a fund raising event ahead of time to help defray costs of the event. (How about selling this book to all of your parents? Contact Lanewood Marketing, (952) 941-7272 to arrange a bulk discount purchase.)
- Ask each graduate to provide a photo of themselves from when they were younger, and mount them with their senior photo in order around the walls. Do this in advance.
- Solicit prize or cash donations from local merchants and thank them in an article or ad in your local paper.

- Try to get a lot of little prizes in stead of huge grand prizes; everyone wants to win something.
- If your facility includes a pool, buy or rent fun rafts for the graduates to play on. Make sure you have lifeguards.

- Be sure to confirm all of your hired professionals the day before the event.
- Organize a volunteer check-in station so volunteers know where to go when they get there. Provide name tags.
- Provide a quiet rest area with cots or inflated mattresses.

Have a good graduation party idea? Send it to us!

# All Night Party Examples

- In Annandale, Virginia the parents work with the school to host an all night party at the local recreation center. The large swimming pool is the center of attention with fun rafts anchored around the pool. Everyone receives a disposable camera when they arrive and fun pictures are taken all night. They have prize drawings throughout the night based on the graduates' assigned numbers being randomly drawn.

  Other rooms in the rec center offer gambling, temporary tattoos, palm reading, boxing on a moon bounce, surf boarding, elastarun (two kids are tethered at the waist to huge rubber bands, and they see who can run the furthest, before being sprung back). They also had a rock climbing wall and a wandering magician. Lots of food and beverages were provided.

- Poly High School in Riverside, California hosted their lock-in at Universal City Walk. The venue included the Hard Rock Café and the 3-D theater where the kids listened to live entertainment. Their favorite performance was by a hypnotist who really got the crowd involved. Dancing the night away for only $70 is a great alternative that keeps the kids safe.

- Eden Prairie High School in Minnesota held their lock-in at the local mall. A band played in the main courtyard while empty store fronts were converted into a coffee and karaoke bar, and a salon with chair massages, makeovers and manicures. There was a gambling club, a hypnotist, and a roving magician. Digital photos were taken of all of the kids and given out that night. They hired a video photographer to capture candid shots and later sold the tapes to the graduates.

# Is Your Graduate Going to College?

College students love getting mail, especially packages from home. If they live in a dorm, the students hang out by the mail boxes, hoping to get something. Whether it's a box of cookies, granola bars, peanuts they can share with their friends, it's fun to receive something from home.

E-mail is great for keeping in touch, but the students don't find that e-mail has the same personal touch that a real letter does. So send them handwritten letters and other fun stuff: local newspaper articles (you could even send them a subscription to the local paper), homemade or their favorite store bought goodies.

Start a "First Year College Mom's Group." It's a good way to keep up the friendships you've developed over the years with other mothers in the school. Now you have a common goal of keeping in touch with your graduates. A fun way to do it is to assemble care packages together. One local group of 10 moms assigns everyone the task of finding 10 little, easy to ship gifts for the kids. They get together once a month and trade gifts and assemble care packages. Some examples include: post it notes, stamps, post cards, new CDs, microwave popcorn, reprints of photos of the students, plastic drinking cups, and snacks, snacks, snacks! Include a list of addresses, phone numbers and e-mail for everyone involved so the graduates can keep in touch. If you have e-mail set up a group mailing list and send group messages out occasionally to encourage them. Send photos out this way as well.

Also, if your college has a parent's weekend, be sure to call early for reservations, they fill up fast.

**Have a good graduation party idea? Send it to us!**

# Appendix

Letter to the graduate from you
Budget
Party planning schedule

# A Letter to the Graduate from You!

Dear Graduate,

Graduation is a major milestone in your life. We are very proud of all your accomplishments: list a few here: for example; grades, academic accomplishments, extracurricular activities, athletic events, friendships formed, good deeds and philanthropic activities.

As we prepare to host a party to honor your achievements and pay tribute to these success, we hope you will remember to thank your guests for being a part of your success. Have a great time!

It is such an exciting time for all of us. It seems like it was just yesterday that you were heading off to kindergarten.

We hope that you enjoyed your years in school and are excited about your future. Next year when you are away at school we hope you will do the best that you can do and remember some of the important values we have taught you, list a few here, for example: honesty, respecting your room mates, take care of yourself, don't do drugs or drink, get enough sleep.

We will always be here for you.

Remember, Celebrate!

We Love You,

Sign your name

Have a good graduation party idea? Send it to us!

# Budget Worksheet

Here is a sample budget for you to fill in the blanks:

Invitations:

       Quantity: _____ x Printing Price _____ =       _____

       Quantity: _____ x Postage _____=       _____

       Waiver from photographer to use photo?       _____

Rental fee for park or party room       _____

Decorations       _____

Entertainment       _____

Tent rental       _____

Table and linen rental       _____

Video tape production or scrap book assembly       _____

Banners and signs       _____

Caterer/Food       _____

Beverages       _____

Hire a food server/helper       _____

Gifts for the graduates       _____

Home improvement  (*Were you going to do it anyway?*)       _____

Cleaning services       _____

Flowers and balloons       _____

Other fun stuff to rent or buy       _____

TOTAL:       _____

*According to the Minneapolis Star Tribune, the average family spends $500 to $2,000 on graduation open houses/parties.*

# The Party Planning Schedule

## Three Months Prior to the Party

- ☐ Check calendar and call school to get schedule of events
- ☐ Decide if you want to co-host with other parents
- ☐ Determine budget
- ☐ Pick date & location
- ☐ Rent tent?
- ☐ Start collecting memorabilia and assembling scrapbook
- ☐ Get bids from video production firms
- ☐ Get bids on home improvements
- ☐ Call caterers or local restaurants for bids
- ☐
- ☐
- ☐

## Two Months Prior to the Party

- ☐ Decide on theme, entertainment
- ☐ Order or start making invitations
- ☐ Start on invitation list
- ☐ Select caterer or ask a friend to help
- ☐ Rent tables, games, serving equipment?
- ☐ Buy paper plates, napkins, silverware, glasses, etc.
- ☐ Buy decorations
- ☐
- ☐
- ☐
- ☐

## One Month Prior to the Party

- ☐ Order food & beverages
- ☐ Mail invitations
- ☐ Schedule carpet cleaner
- ☐ Buy gifts for graduate and friends
- ☐ Find a place for your pets
- ☐ Finish scrapbook
- ☐ Meet with caterer to finalize plans
- ☐
- ☐
- ☐

**Have a good graduation party idea? Send it to us!**

# Down to the Wire

## One Week Prior to the Party

- ☐ Pick up food & beverages
- ☐ Buy extra film and batteries and charge video batteries
- ☐ Send invitations to school with your graduate
- ☐ Clean house and decorate
- ☐ Wrap gifts for graduate and friends
- ☐ Make card holder and set up memorabilia
- ☐ Label recycling containers
- ☐ Confirm hotel reservations for out of town guests
- ☐ Write last minute "to do" list
- ☐ Set up tent on the day before the party
- ☐ Review guest list and expectations with graduate.
- ☐

**Scott's Party!**

## On the day of the party:

- ☐ Sleep as late as you can; you're gonna need all the energy you can get!
- ☐ Wake up your graduate with breakfast in bed.
- ☐ Take your pet to a friend's for a day of rest.
- ☐ Review your own "to do" list.
- ☐ Water the plants and flowers.
- ☐ Sweep the front entry way, driveway and garage (if you are using it).
- ☐ Make sure everything looks nice from the street.
- ☐ Put up yard signs and directional signs.
- ☐ Set out non-perishable food early.
- ☐ Set out perishable food at the last minute.
- ☐ Set tables.
- ☐ Set out trash barrels (and recycling boxes if serving canned drinks).
- ☐ Set out the tables and chairs.
- ☐ Put table clothes on tables.
- ☐ Consider weather issues, i. e. Do you have enough shade? Windy?
- ☐ Give your graduate a letter saying how proud you are of them.
- ☐ **Give your graduate a big hug and let the celebration begin!**

# We need your input for our next edition!

Have you found this book to be helpful?

Did you have a few unanswered questions?

Did we make you laugh or cry?

Did you come up with a few suggestions of your own?

What have we overlooked?

What can we do better?

Whether you wait until you've had your party or not, please write to us at 11330 Lanewood Circles, Eden Prairie, MN 55344. Or send us email at mary@graduationparty.com Or call Mary at (952) 941-7272

# To order additional copies for a friend!

To order additional copies of this book send $9.95 + $2 for shipping to:     Lanewood Marketing

11330 Lanewood Circles

Eden Prairie, MN 55344.

Include the mailing address you would like the book sent to.

**Have a good graduation party idea? Send it to us!**

# Notes

# Notes